THE GOLFERS

Carving with Tom Wolfe

Text written with
Douglas Congdon-Martin

Schiffer Publishing Ltd

1469 Morstein Road, West Chester, Pennsylvania 19380

Published by Schiffer Publishing, Ltd.
1469 Morstein Road
West Chester, Pennsylvania 19380
Please write for a free catalog.
This book may be purchased from the publisher.
Please include $2.00 postage.
Try your bookstore first.

Printed in the United States of America.
ISBN: 0-88740-293-3

We are interested in hearing from authors with book
ideas on related topics.

Contents

Introduction

"This ever happened to you?" he asked me.

"Yep," I said.

"What did you do?"

"Played it out."

He stared at me in disbelief. "Played it out? How did you do that?"

"I just went to the car and got a tire iron."

Of course golfing has an international following of both players and spectators. One story suggests that is also has a heavenly following.

It seems that the Lord is also a golfer. One time he came to Pinehurst to play eighteen holes. Gabriel caddied for him. On one par five the Lord found himself about 200 yards from the green.

"Give me a nine iron," he said to Gabriel.

Being a good caddy, Gabriel suggested, "You'll never make it with a nine iron. It's too far."

"What do you mean 'too far'?" said the Lord. "Just last week I saw Arnold Palmer make exactly this same shot, and he used a nine iron."

"But..."

"Just give me the nine iron," said the Lord, getting a bit perturbed.

Another golfer had came along and saw what was happening. While the Lord addressed the ball, the golfer pulled Gabriel aside.

"He'll never make it with a nine iron. Who does he think he is, Jesus Christ?" he asked.

"He knows he's Jesus Christ," Gabriel answered, "He thinks he's Arnold Palmer."

Well, you don't have to be Jesus Christ or Arnold Palmer to do projects in this book They require only a few simple carving tools, and are perfect for the advanced beginner and intermediate carver while still presenting a challenge to the veteran. We have taken the carving of one of the foursome of golfers and gone step-by-step through the process using full-color pictures to show clearly what must be done and how to do it. With that experience and the patterns included at the beginning of the book, the carver should be able to complete the set with little difficulty. I hope you have fun with these projects.

Those who golf are a dedicated sort. My dad is 80 years old and legally blind. But everyday it isn't raining or snowing he's out on the links. He can still hit the ball well. He just needs someone to line him up, and he can drive it a mile. That's the way it is with golfers.

I suppose there is something of my father in the golfers I carved for this book. They have all been around the course a few times, and wouldn't miss it for the world. I have known them or people like them all my life.

I guess that's why it is hard to categorize the carving in *The Golfers*. It is not caricature and it is not realism. Rather it is what I like to call exaggerated realism. The four golfers shown in this book are characters who are believable, but their features are exaggerated slightly to give them life.

North Carolina is the golf capital of the world. The Golfing Hall of Fame is located in Pinehurst and it is the home of several major tournaments. With the strong Scotch-Irish presence in the area it is still possible to see some old golfers traversing the links in kilts.

Down here there's a golf course on top of Seven Devils Mountain. In the winter the wind gets so bad up there that it blows all the sand off the traps. They've taken to using old used tires to keep the sand in place. From late fall until early spring the sand traps are covered.

One spring my boy and I were playing the Seven Devils course with two Yankees. One of them hit his ball smack in the middle of one of those tires. He stood there staring at the ball and shaking his head.

The Tools and Patterns

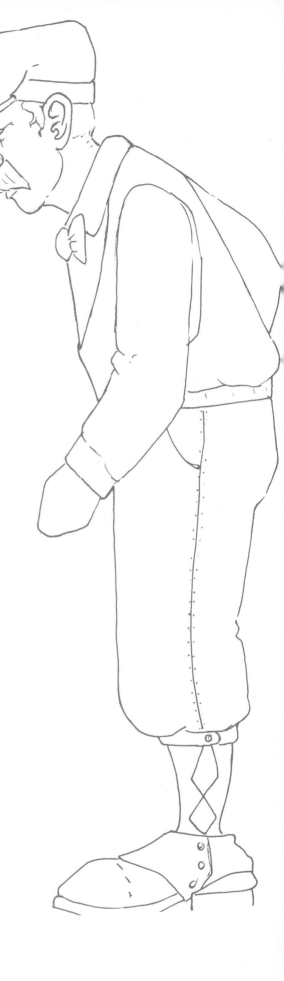

The tools needed for this project include a simple set of palm gouges, a turned-down blade and a turned-up blade. The wood I use is bass, and that is probably the best for these figures. It carves well and takes the paint nicely.

The block used for the body is 4 inches wide, 10 inches tall and 4 inches deep. For the head I used a block 4 inches long, 3 inches wide and 2½ inches deep. If you decide on a different size, you can use a photocopying machine with the capacity to enlarge or reduce to make the pattern any size you want. The copying machine can also be used to make several copies of the pattern, which you can then cut apart as needed to help in drawing various parts of the figure.

The patterns may be combined and mixed in a variety of ways to make the golfer pose in almost any position you please. He could be driving the ball, or putting, or throwing his club into the water in a moment of frustration. You may use the head of one pattern and the body of another, or the top of one body and the bottom of another. The hands in the patterns are drawn without details, so you can carve them to fit the use you have for them, whether holding a club or a score card, or waving a fist in the air.

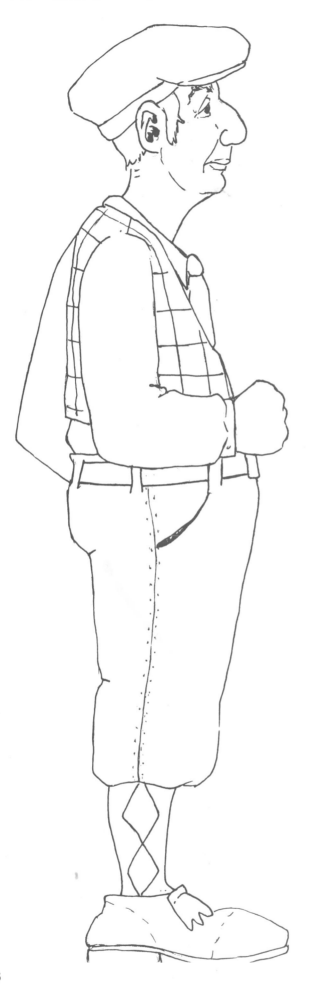

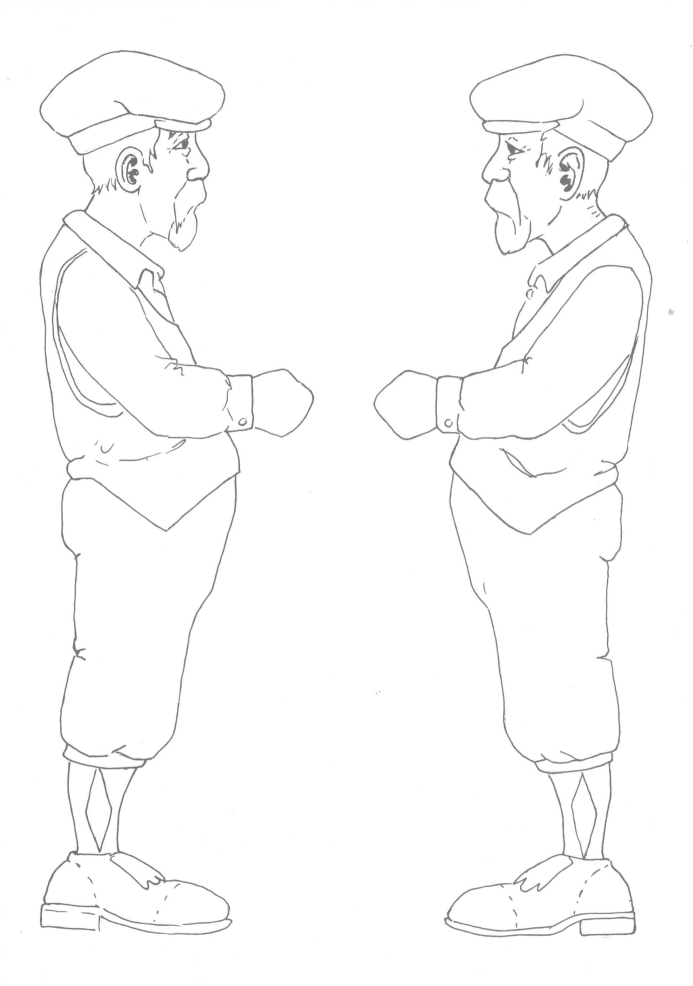

Carving the Golfer

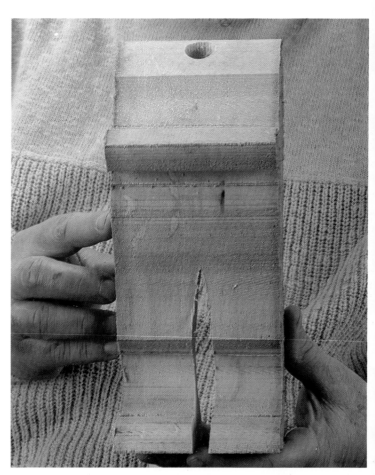

Cut out the body and head on a band saw.

There is no frontal pattern for the body, because there is a big danger of over cutting. It easier and leads to a better result when you carve away the excess wood to form the figure, instead of trying to match a pattern.

Because the neck tapers toward the bottom, this bottom measurement determines the size drill bit I use for the neck hole. I use a flat bit to drill the hole.

Drill a hole where the head will be inserted into the body.

Begin by trimming the sides of the neck, working from the head to the base.

Trim and round the neck until the base is rounded to the diameter of the profile. Do not over cut.

When it is fairly round, insert the head in the neck hole and twist the head in the socket.

This will create shiny, smooth spots where the neck has high points. These should be trimmed and the process repeated until the neck is smooth all over.

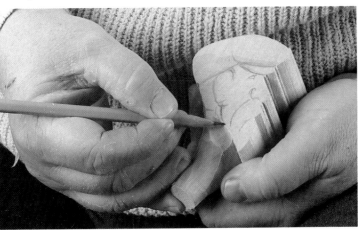

Before finishing the neck trimming, mark the facial features so you can define the chin line and other features and don't cut them away by mistake.

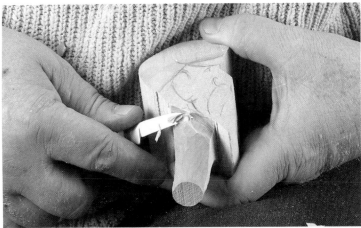

Cut down to the neck line from the ear and chin. The neck should be distinct and tapering. Place the head in the body and repeat the twisting action often to be sure you are not cutting too much away from the neck. If the neck fits well you will be able to turn the head to look any way you wish when finishing the figure.

This is how the properly fitted neck and head will fit in the body.

Cut straight in to put some stops around the bottom of the hat...

and cut back into them.

Draw a center line all the way around the head.

Trim away the corners of the face. A common mistake here is not trimming off enough, leaving a flat-faced figure. Trim until it looks right...then trim a little more.

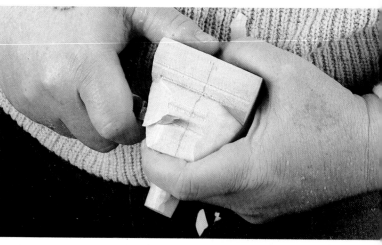

This will give you some idea how far to go.

Draw the width of the nose. Make sure it is wide enough for the nostril. Another common mistake is to cut the nose too thin.

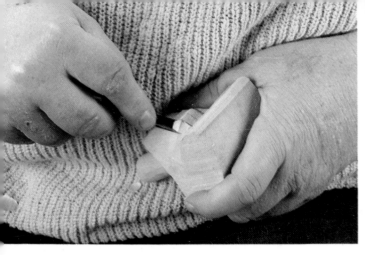

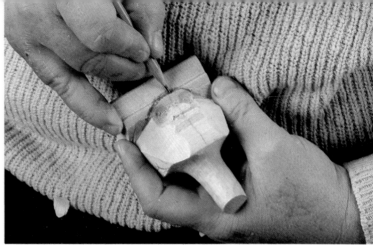

I use a gouge to carve facial features. It gives a rounded effect and prevents making sharp indentions around the eyes and nose. Start around the nostril.

Draw a curve in the bill of the golfer's cap. This will give more room for the forehead and eyebrows.

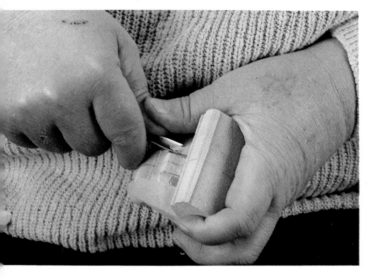

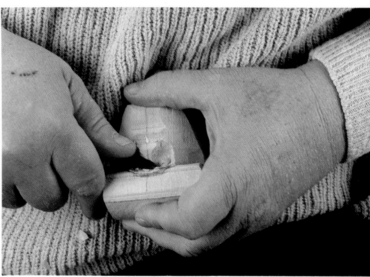

I lock in the gouge by using both hands. This prevents accidental cuts to the piece and to my hands. I push with my right hand while applying counter-pressure with the thumb of my left hand. This always gives me a control position for my work.

Use a knife to cut a stop at the forehead, so you will not cut into the face.

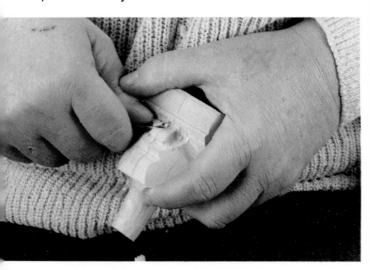

Gouge the eye sockets, going with the grain from the outside of the face to the bridge of the nose.

Carve away the wood under the bill of the cap using a gouge.

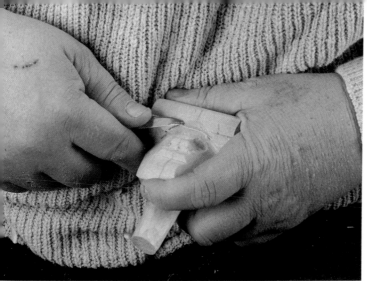

With a knife cut a thin line above the bill to define its thickness.

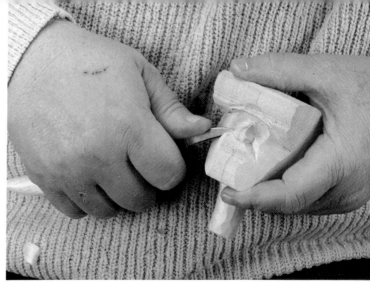

Cut a stop on the line down the cheek...

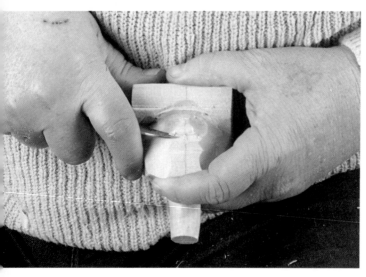

Returning to the nose, note that the nostrils flare upwards from the center. Cut a wedge from the bottom of the nose on each side to mark this flare.

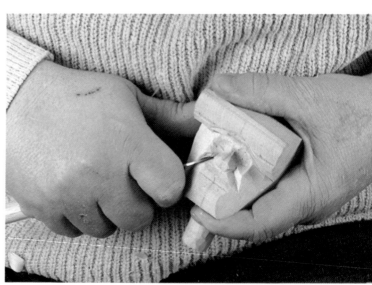

and cut back into it from the moustache. This will bring out the lip, moustache, and the cheek.

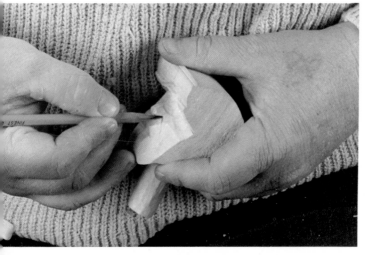

This golfer has a Van Dyke moustache and beard. The moustache line follows the cheek line, coming a little higher than the bottom of the nose. Draw the line.

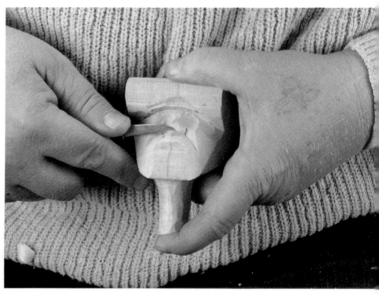

Clean up and further define the nose.

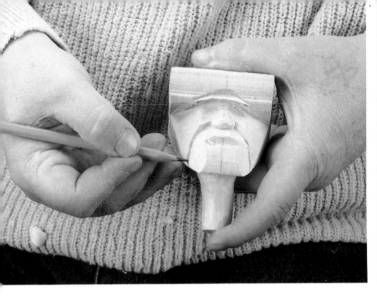

Mark the moustache running down into the beard in the Van Dyke way.

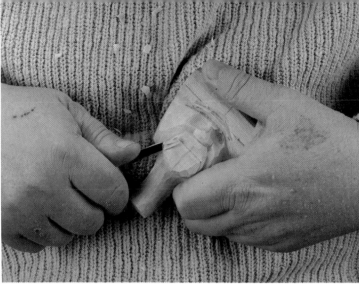

Cut a stop on this lower moustache line and trim the beard back to it.

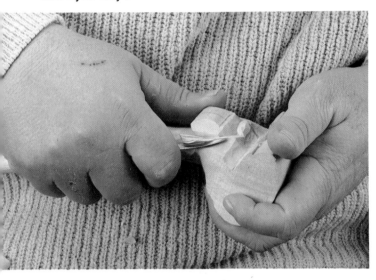

After making a stop, trim the face down to the beard line, bringing out the Van Dyke.

The beard and moustache will look like this.

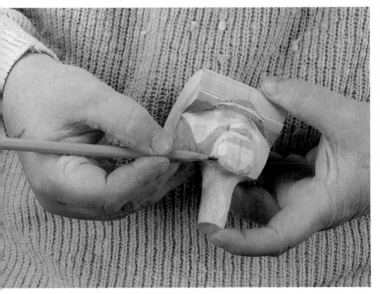

Mark a line for the bottom edge of the moustache.

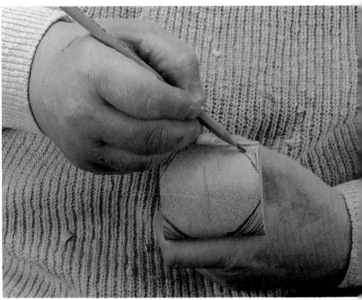

Mark the top of the cap to give it the round look.

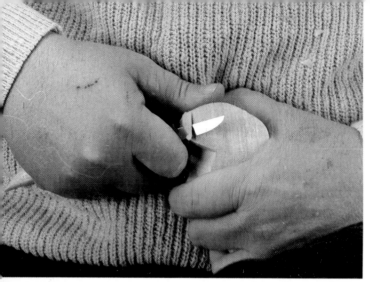

Trim the corners. They should just pop off.

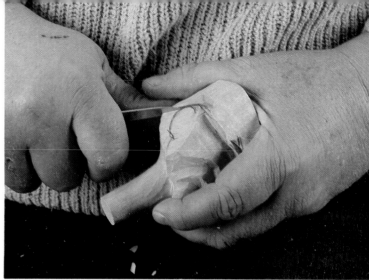

The ear will be carved out first to be sure it comes outside and over the line of the cap. Carve out a v-chip to leave the line of the ear and the line of the cap distinct and clear.

With the corners trimmed the cap will look like this from the top.

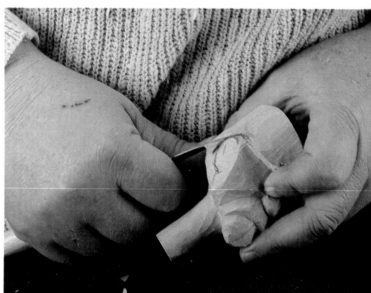

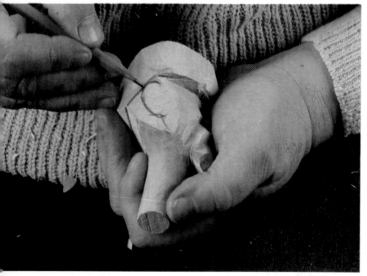

Using the pattern as a guide, draw the lines on the cap and the top of the ear.

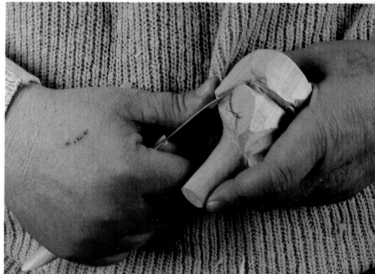

Trim the excess behind and above the ear.

Use the gouge to silhouette the ear and trim down to the neck.

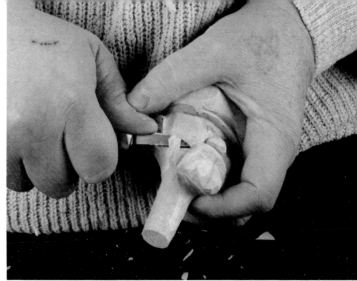

Carve away the cheek.

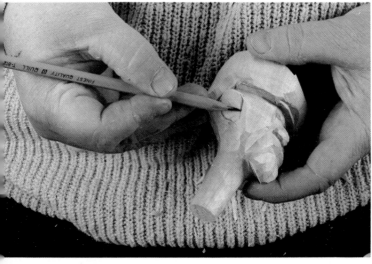

Draw a line for the sideburn in front of the ear.

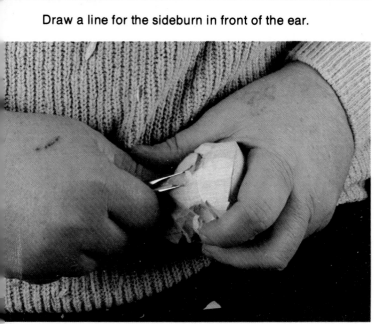

Trim away the sideburn area in front of the ear. Leave the ear protruding for now.

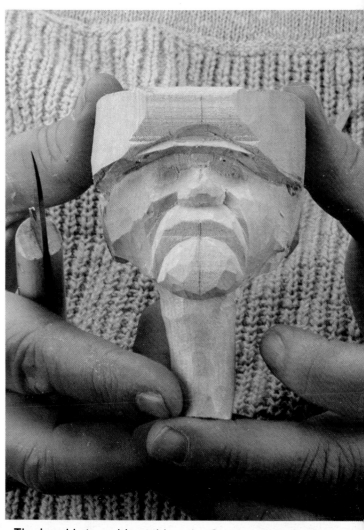

The head is too wide at this point. Starting with the face and leaving the ears and cap until last, we begin to carve away some of the width. Leaving the ears will give much more design flexibility later in the carving, allowing you to decide whether they flare out, are flat, or whatever. The ears and nose give the face its character, so they are important to the overall design.

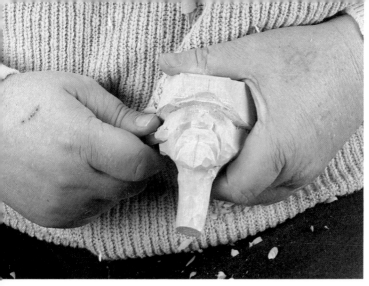

Use the gouge and go from side to side to keep things symmetrical.

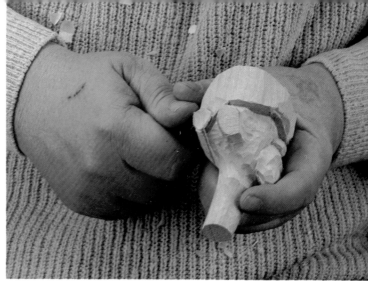

Taper the cap down the back of the head and into the neck.

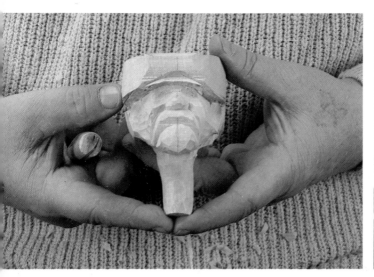

The face begins to take on a better proportion.

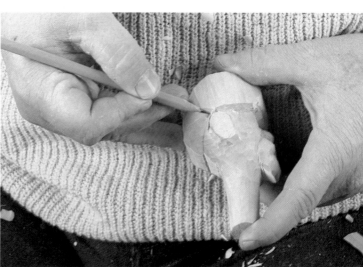

Redraw the line of the cap.

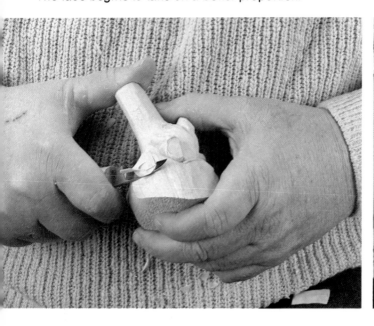

After thinning the face, shape the cap.

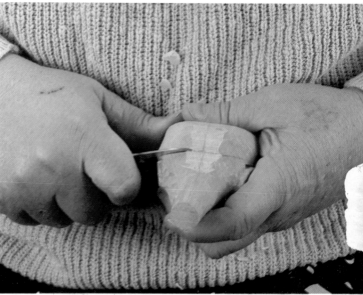

Cut a stop around the bottom of the cap line.

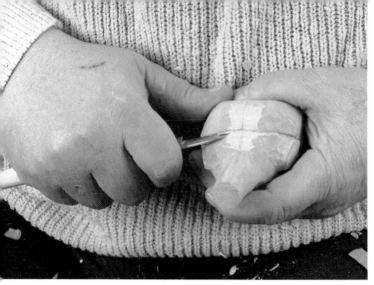

Trim the neck back to the stop.

Mark the continuation of the bill around the side of the cap.

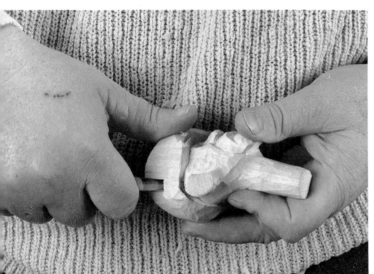

Taper the side of the cap into the head above the ears.

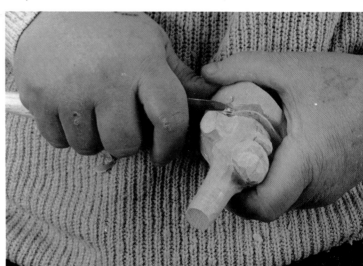

By making a stop and carving back to it from the cap, make a v-groove to mark the top of the bill.

Cut a stop along the line of the cap to maintain its shape while you trim it.

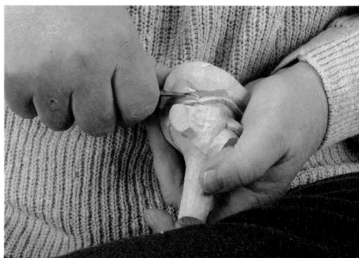

To get the effect of the cap being more blousey in the front than the sides, cut in fold marks at the back of the bill.

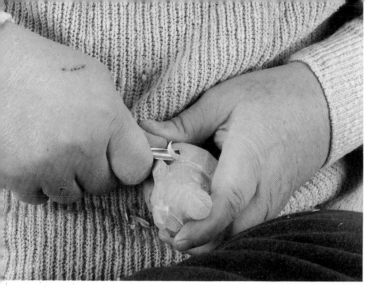

To make the band around the back of the cap, go around the bottom edge with the gouge.

By trimming the front top of the cap on the two sides, we give it the well-worn look we are after.

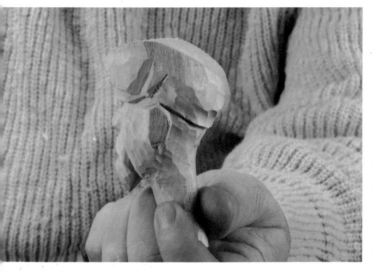

The back of the cap

Now to carve the ears we begin by using a gouge to give them their overall shape.

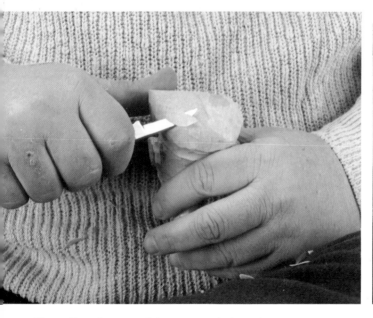

Round up the top of the cap and clean it up.

Smooth and give further shape using a knife.

Draw in the sideburns.

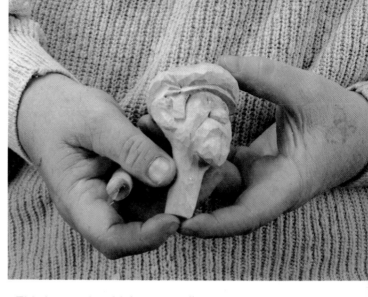

This leaves the sideburn standing out.

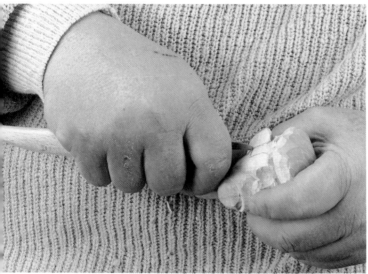

Cut a stop all around the sideburns.

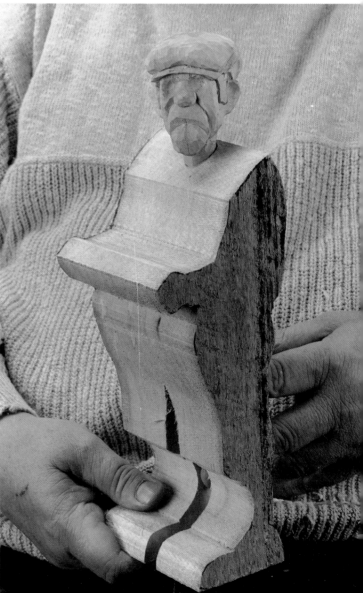

Cut into the stop with the gouge, going all around the sideburns.

A trial fitting. Doing this occasionally helps keep the piece in perspective.

Mark the nostril location.

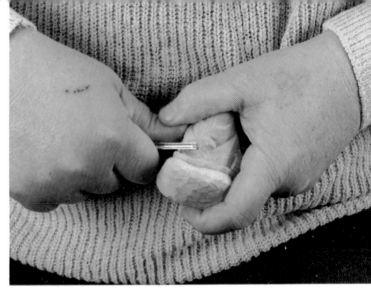

Shape the nose above the nostril using a gouge and knife. This gives the figure much of its character.

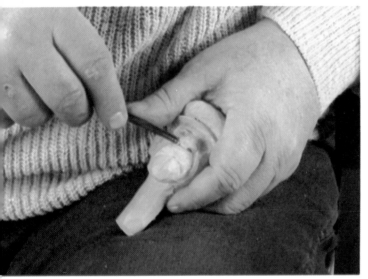

Using a smaller gouge push straight in around the nostril hole.

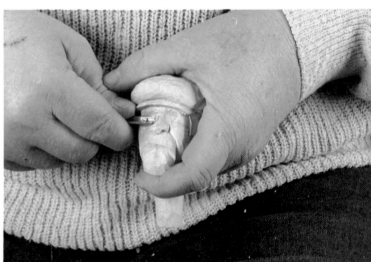

Shape the corners of the eyes with a gouge.

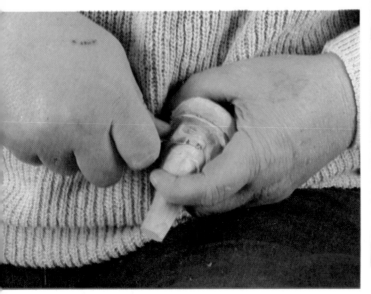

Clean the hole with a knife.

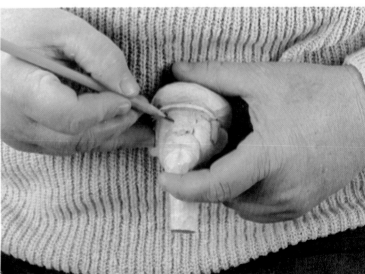

Mark the center of the eyes. Usually the center of the eyes are directly above the corners of the mouth, so visualize a line to locate the pupils.

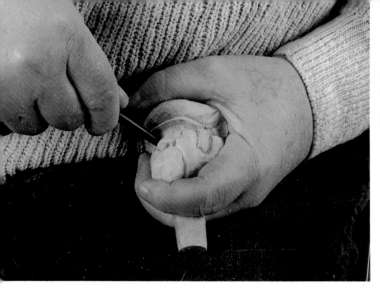

Use a large nailset to define the iris. Do the left eye first, holding the head upside down. Push the nailset in and twist.

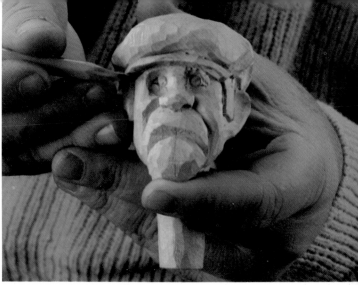

Mark the slits in the eyes. The character will be determined by these lines. Down denotes seriousness, up gives a feeling of happiness.

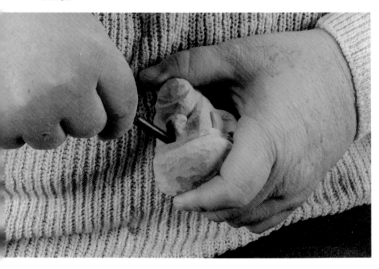

When you turn the head around to do the right, it will be easier to line up the two eyes, and make sure they are correct.

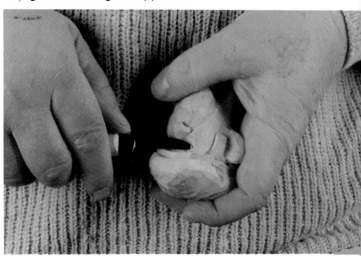

Use the very tip of the knife form the outer corners of the upper and lower eyelids. Come in at an extreme angle so the eyeball is formed by the cut.

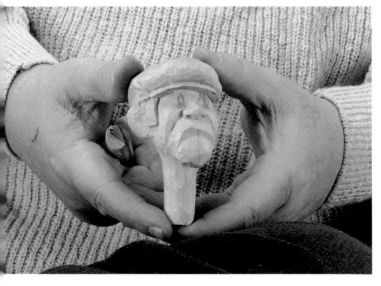

The eyes so far.

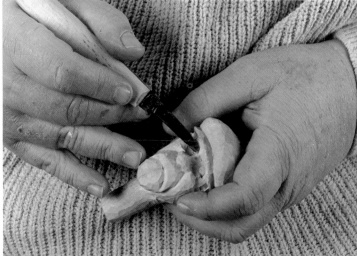

Do the same thing to form the inside corners of the eyelids.

Use the gouge to give detail to the lower eyelids.

The finished eyes.

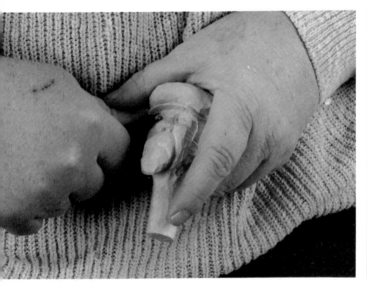

Then do the same on the top.

Clean up the head carving, then mark the inside of the ear with a swirl at the top...

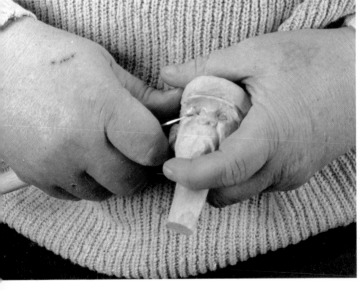

The eyes look too hollow, so we'll trim some wood from the outside corner, opening it up a little.

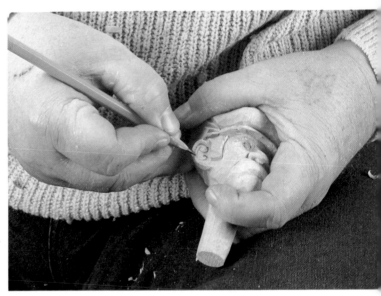

and another, opposite swirl at the bottom.

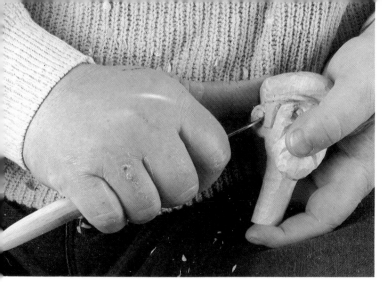

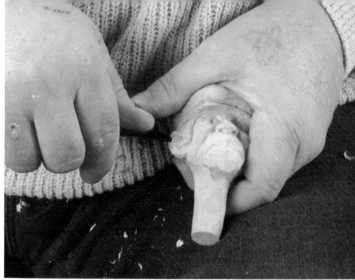

Carve away the outer line until it tapers out toward the bottom of the ear.

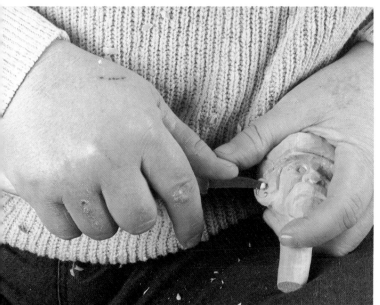

Use a knife to chip out the marked areas top...

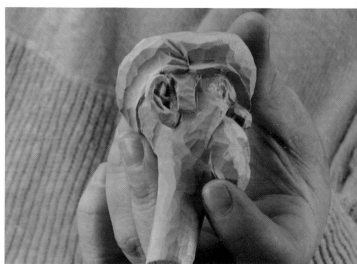

The finished ear.

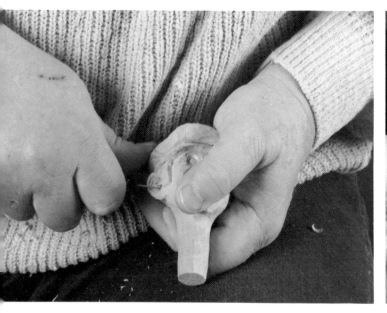

and bottom.

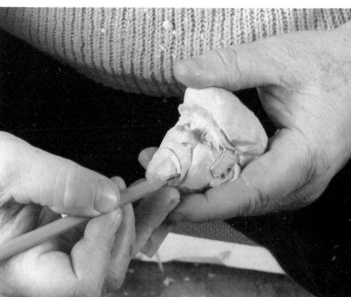

Draw in the bottom edge of the moustache...

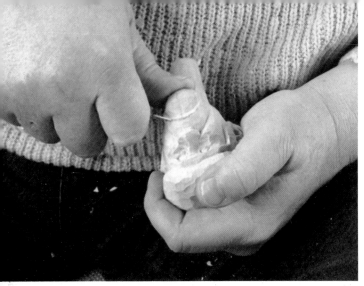

and carve a stop into it.

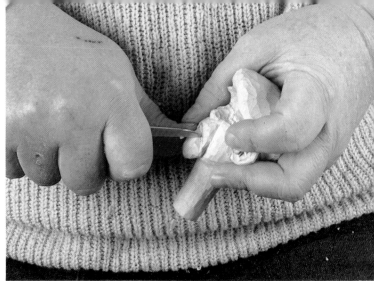

Cut a stop at the corner marks and carve into it with a small gouge from the side.

Cut back to the stop from just a little bit below, creating a bottom lip

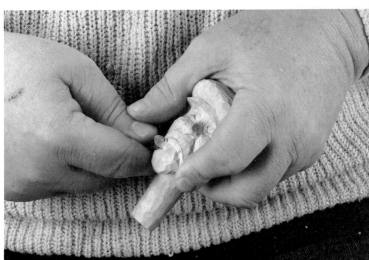

Use a large gouge to make the indentation below the bottom lip.

Mark the corners of the mouth. Remember it should line up with the pupils of the eyes.

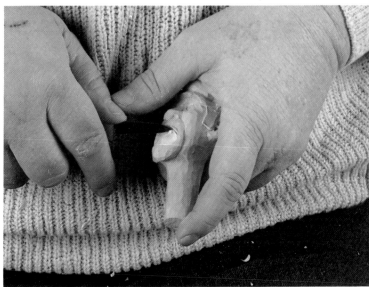

Use a knife to round the corners of the lips.

The finished head.

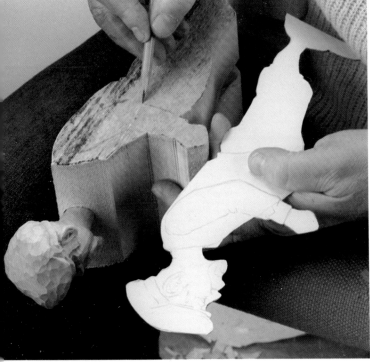

After deciding on the pose of the golfer, mark the arms. Use the pattern as a guide.

Cut a stop along the lines of the arm...

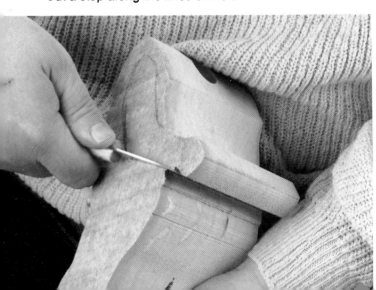

and carve back to it.

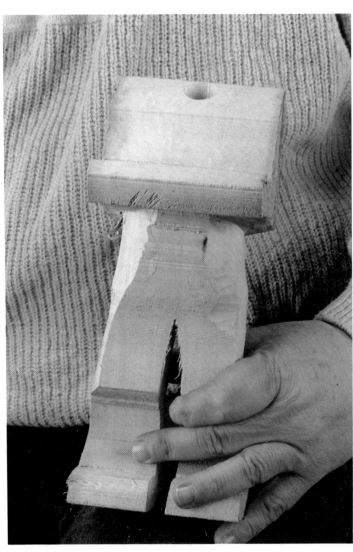

Carve away the excess wood from the lower body up to the arm. Trim all around to the size of the waist.,

25

Remove excess wood from behind the arm.

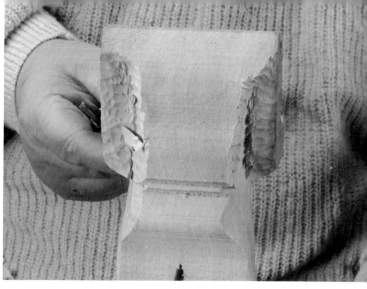

This is the back view after removing the wood behind the arms.

This is best done with a gauge, holding it in the palm and cutting toward yourself.

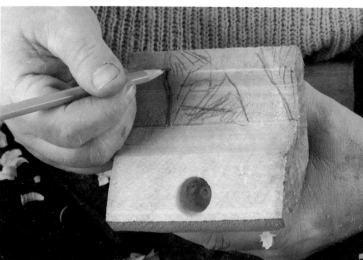

Mark the inside of the arms. The right arm which will hold the pencil will turn in more than the left. Otherwise the figure will seem stiff and lifeless. This will make the right arm longer, so an adjustment will have to be made to the elbow later.

Pop off the excess material on the outside of the arm. This is possible because of the grain. Any time you can take advantage of the grain it will reduce the carving time and effort.

Clean up the area behind the arm with a gouge.

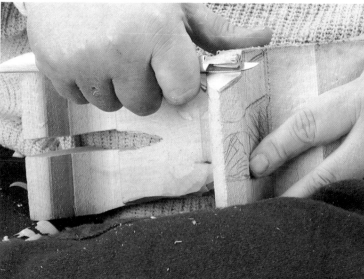

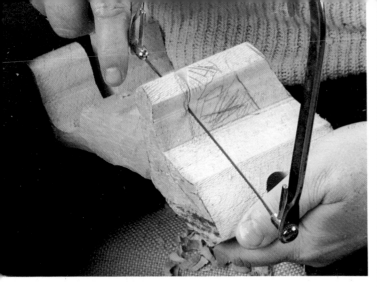

Use a coping saw to cut the lines of the inside of the arms. This saves a lot of time.

Clean out any remaining wood between the arms with a knife.

Push and pry the center piece from the top and bottom with a gouge...

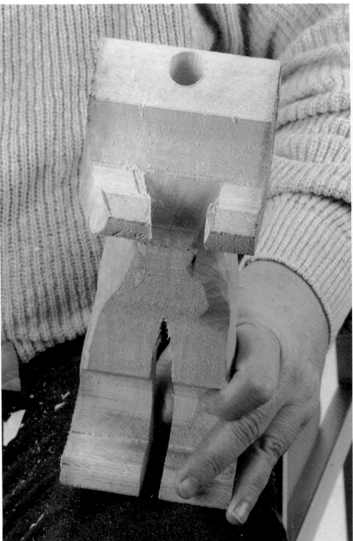

until it pops out.

The roughed-out body.

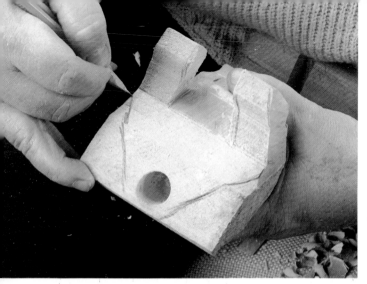

Mark the rounded-off shoulders.

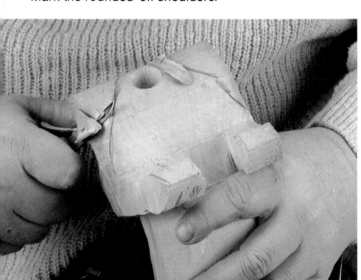

Remove the excess wood from the shoulders, rounding off to the lines.

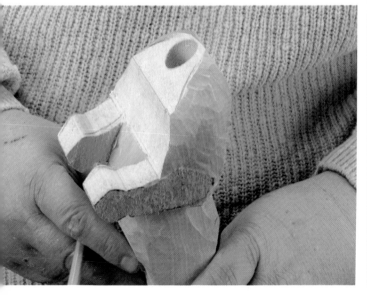

The rounded shoulders

Mark the right arm to make the elbow come forward.

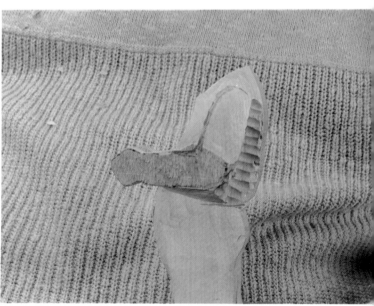

The left arm has the elbow further back.

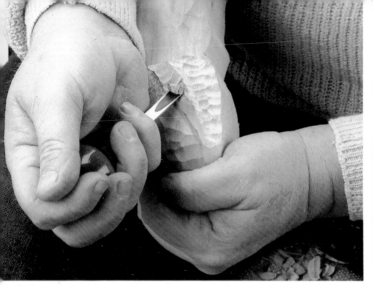

Trim away more wood from behind the right arm.

And the calves and shoes.

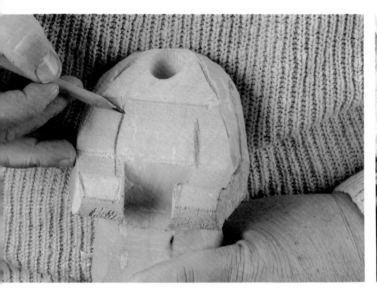

Mark reference lines on the fronts of the arms.

I want the right foot turned at more of an angle than the left foot. So I mark the position on the bottom of the feet, beginning with a center line for each foot...

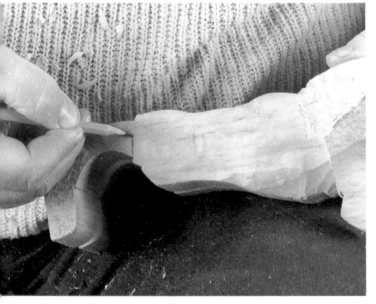

Mark the bottom of the knickers...

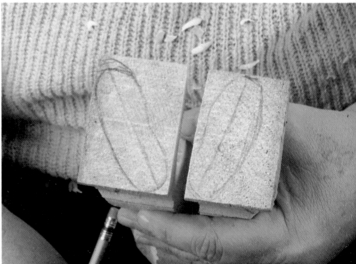

then with the soles of the shoes.

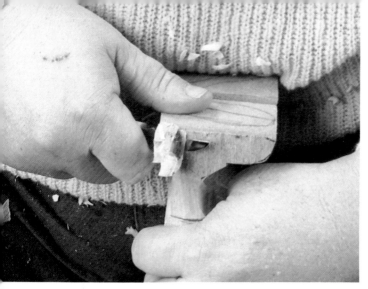

Pop off the excess wood around the sole.

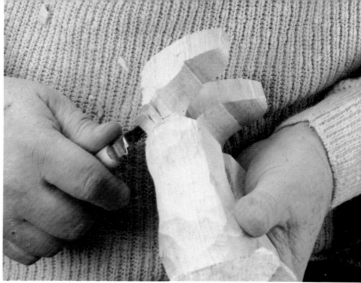

Taper toward the ankles.

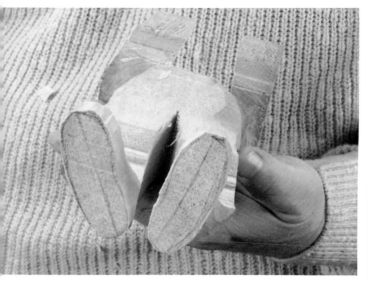

The roughed-out feet.

Then cut from the top of the shoe up the leg until the calf is well-shaped.

Round off the calves under the knickers. Begin by cutting a stop at the bottom of the knickers and carving the leg toward it.

One leg done, one to go.

Clean up the leg as you go.

Round the feet to make them look more like shoes.

Mark the top of the shoes.

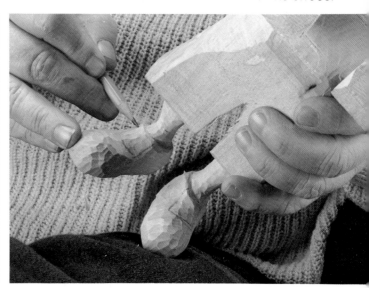

Draw the flaps of the shoes.

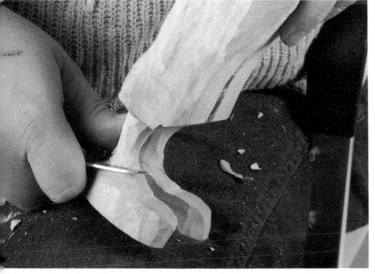

Cut a shallow stop at the top of the shoe and cut into it slightly from the calf to give the impression of the sock going into the shoe.

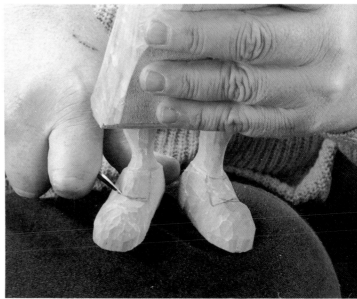

Cut a stop around the flap and trim the shoe up to it.

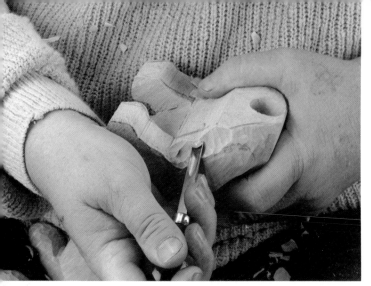

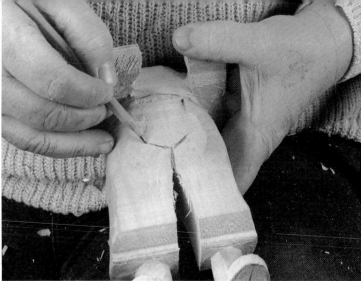

Moving back to the torso, work on the front of the arm by removing excess wood.

and the crotch in the front.

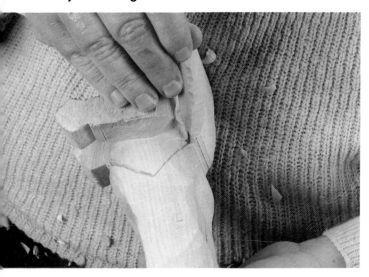

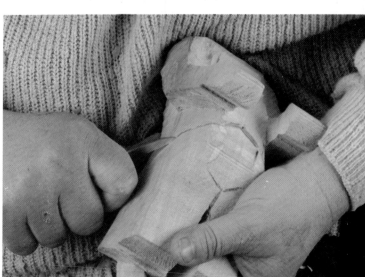

Draw the sweater vest.

Cut a stop along the sweater vest line and cut back to it from the knickers.

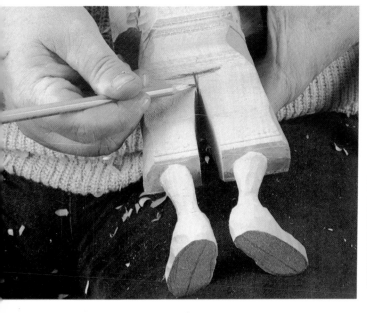

Mark in some details like the crotch in the back...

Cut stops in the V of the front crotch and carve up the legs back to them.

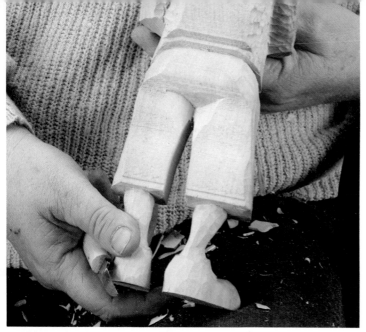

The back is cut similarly.

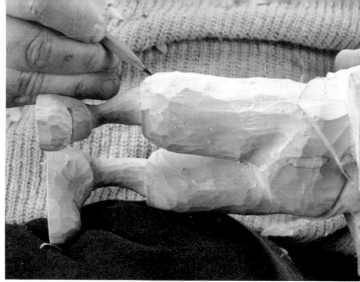

Draw the cuff of the knickers.

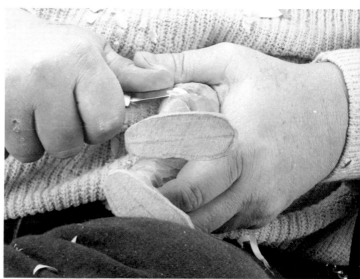

Nip it off from the cuff line toward the foot.

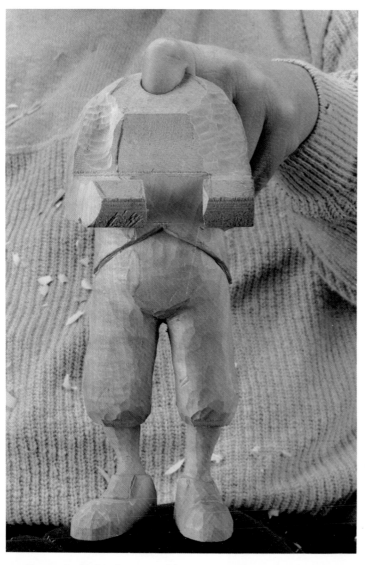

Round off the legs to this point, where the knickers are near completion.

Draw the clothing features, beginning with the shirt and sweater lines

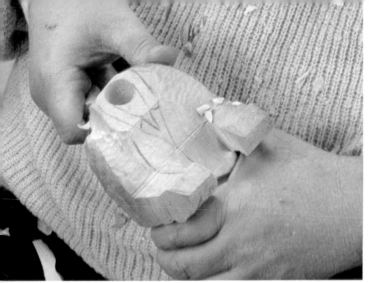

To make the collar stand up it is necessary to cut down on the shoulder.

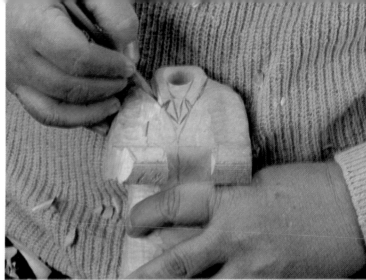

Draw in the details of the collar.

Round the edge of the neck hole.

Make stop cuts in the neckline and cut back to them. The open space will be the t-shirt.

This helps it look more natural and less like a hole drilled and a head stuck in.

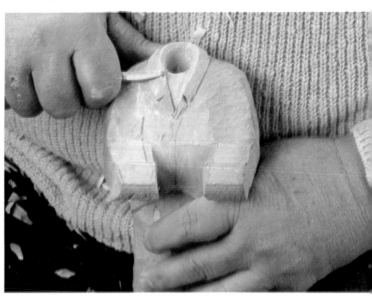

Trim and shape the collar area.

Trim down the upper arms to make the upper body narrower.

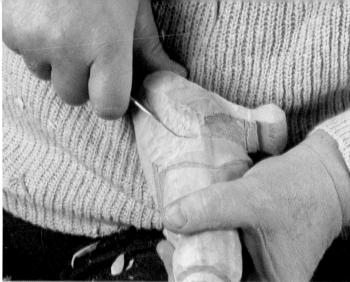

Do the same on both arms.

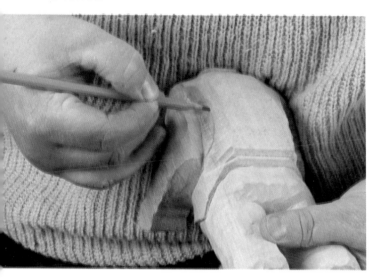

Mark the sleeve opening of the sweater vest.

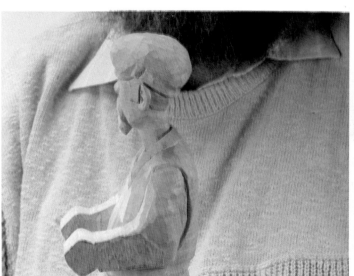

Put the head in place and see how things look. In this case the neck seems a little long...

Cut a stop into the line and cut back to it from the arm, defining the arm pit area.

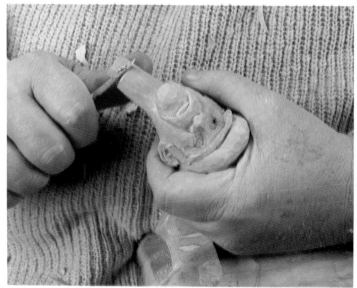

so we take a little bit off at a time...

until it looks just right. The twist and trim method for fitting the neck in the hole will probably need to be used again.

Round the sleeve.

Mark and shape the forearms.

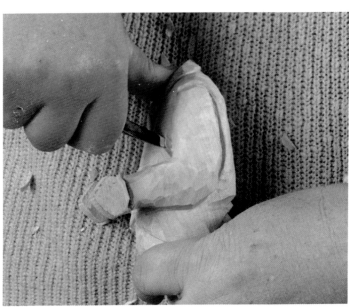

The golf club can go under either arm. In this case it looks better under the left arm. Carve away a little before drilling a hole for the golf club.

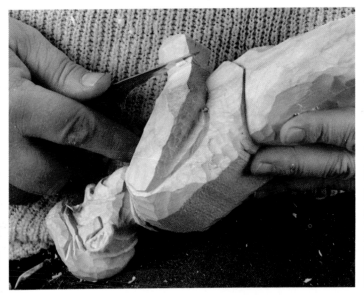

Using the sleeve mark in the blank, trim the wrist to the cuff, leaving the hand blocky for now.

Keep narrowing the arms little by little until they take the shape that looks best.

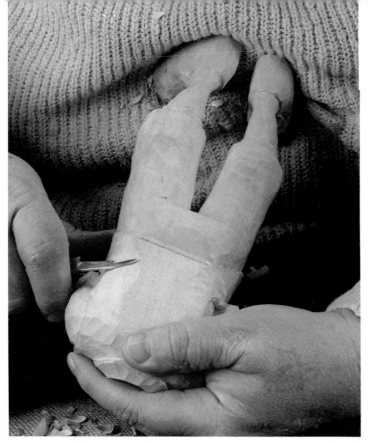

Refine the carving as you go.

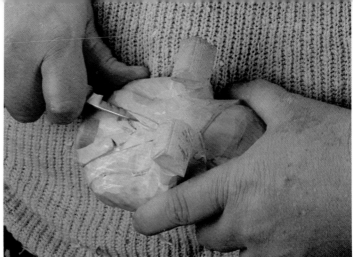

Cut a stop on the line and trim into it from the shirt.

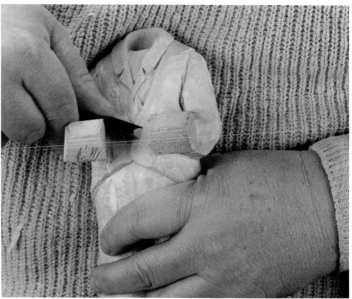

Use a gouge to cut two small depressions for the button hole. Be sure it's on the correct side of the sweater vest.

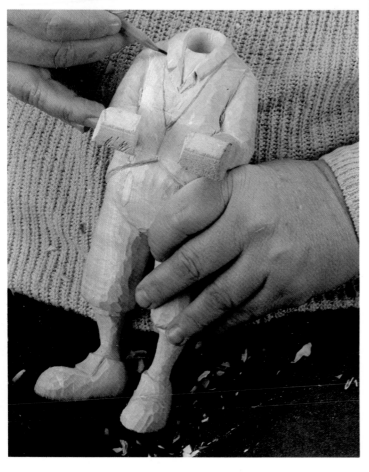

The vest opening in front needs to go a little lower.

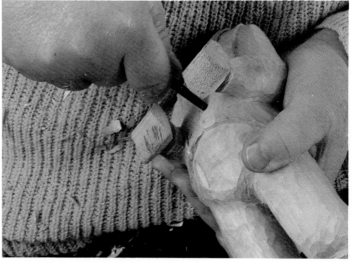

Use a nailset to form the buttons by pushing and twisting as you did for the eyes.

A smaller gouge carving back into the button, creates a wrinkle in the sweater.

Carve into the lines with a v-cut.

Do another button on the shirt.

Mark the fly and top of the knickers.

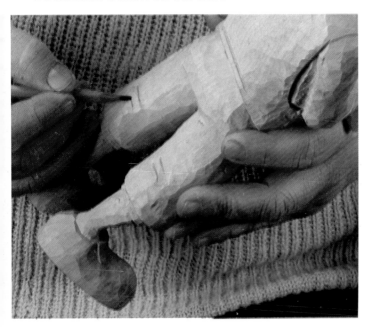

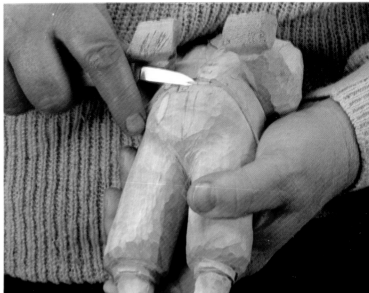

Mark some folds behind the knees

Cut a stop on the top line of the knickers and cut down to it.

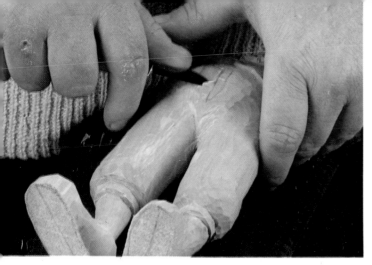

Do the same on the remainder of the closure and on the opening side of the fly.

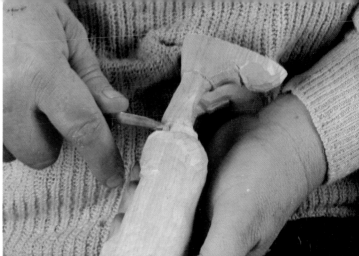

Make a flap at the bottom of the knickers' leg by cutting a straight cut and coming back to it.

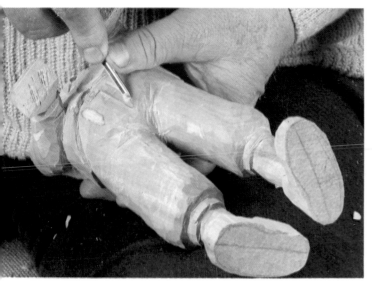

On the seamed side of the fly carve a shallow line with a veiner.

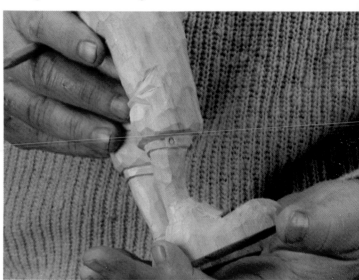

Make a smaller button using a smaller nailset.

Make the button on the knickers in the same way as before.

Mark the heals of the shoes.

Since the figure will be on a stand it is only necessary to nick out a corner of the heel.

Cut down the shoe to the stop forming the indentation above the sole.

Mark the edge of the sole.

Draw lines for seams in the knickers.

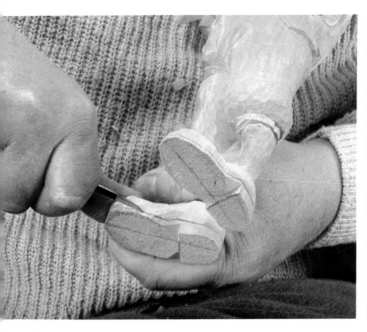

Cut a stop on the sole line.

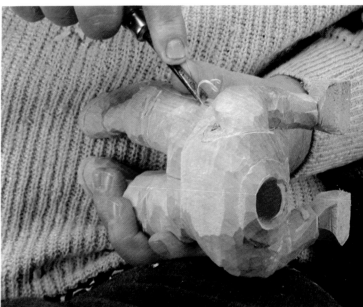

Follow the line with a veiner, making a shallow line.

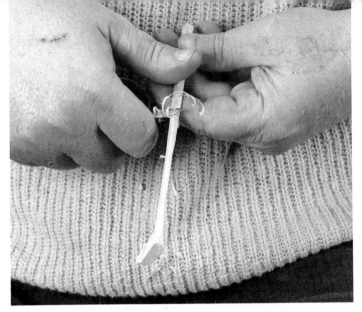

Carve the golf club from the blank

Paying close attention to how you would hold a pencil, draw the right hand of the golfer.

Sand the club smooth.

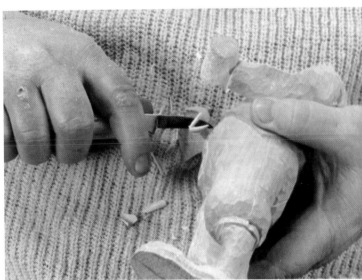

Rough out the general shape of the hand.

Drill a hole into which the club will fit. Visualize where the club will be on the figure. Stop occasionally and look to be sure the angle and placement is right.

Choose the appropriate size drill by holding it up to the model to see if it is right diameter for a pencil. Drill through the hand.

After drilling the pencil hole, draw in the fingers.

Carve a pencil from a small piece of scrap.

Separate the fingers by carving small v-cuts between them.

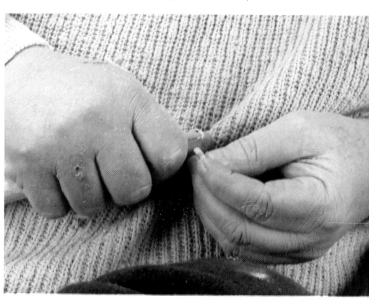

Trim to fit in hole you have drilled.

Use the gouge between the knuckles to give them form.

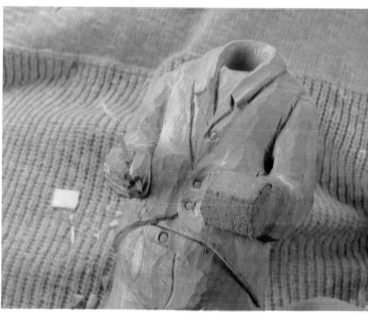

Insert the pencil in the hand.

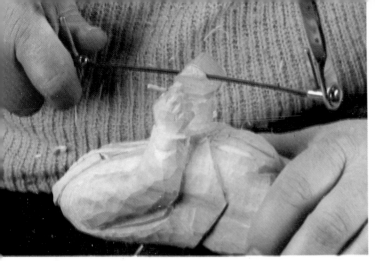

Use a coping saw to make two parallel cuts which will form a slit to hold the scorecard in the left hand. Remove the wood between the two cuts.

and remove the excess.

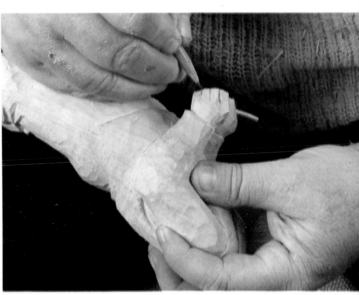

Carve the thumb.

Draw the fingers on the left hand.

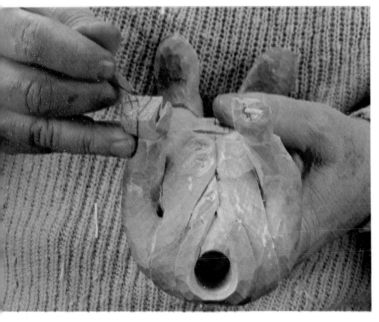

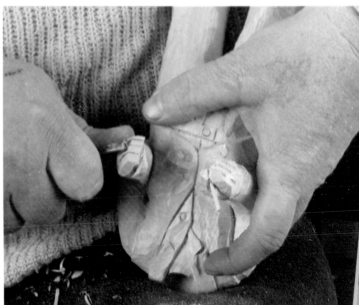

Draw the back of the hand...

Separate the fingers with a veiner.

You can deepen the finger separation with a knife.

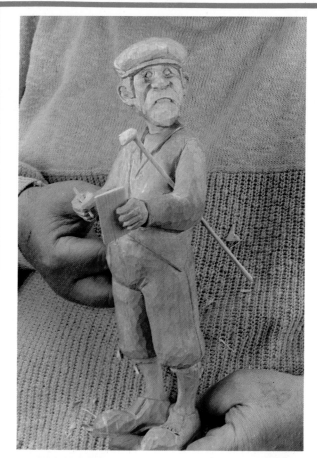

Split the scorecard from a piece of wood and cut it to size with a coping saw.

Clean the scorecard with the knife.

Several views of the assembled, unpainted piece.

Go over the figure smoothing and checking for missing details. The shirt of the score keeper needs a cuff line. Draw it and cut a stop.

Cut the cuff back to the stop.

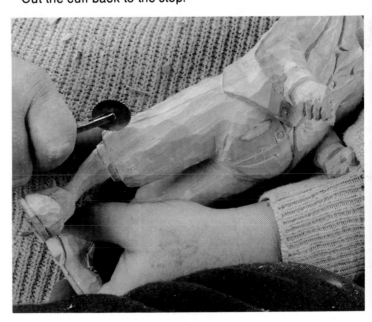

Use a tracing wheel to mark the seam on the knickers. Do all of the seams...

including those around the sleeves...

and the sewing marks on the shoes.

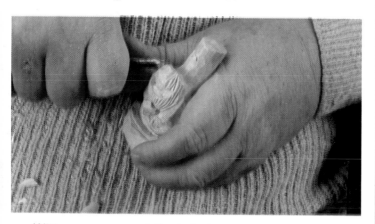

With a v-gouge put the hair details in the moustache, beard, sideburns, and the back of the head.

Ready to paint.

Painting the Golfer

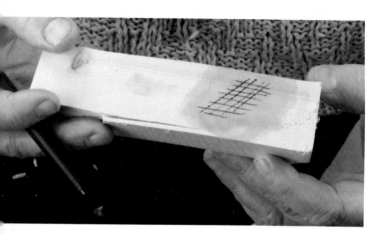

Use a pen to do some of the designs in the fabric. I often use a Flair™ pen, but others will do. Test any pen (the Flair™ will run with a water based paint) first to be sure it won't fade or run with the paint you are using. Mark several lines on a piece of scrap and paint over them with your paints to see what happens.

Mark a striped design on the shirt. Begin by drawing a middle stripe on each sleeve and work out to the sides...

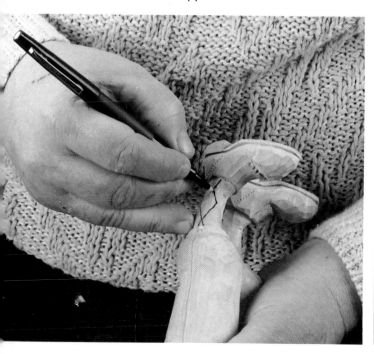

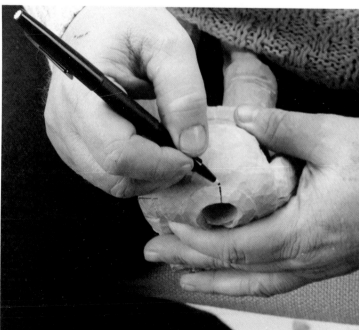

Mark the argyle pattern on the sock.

then draw the middle stripe on the back of the collar.

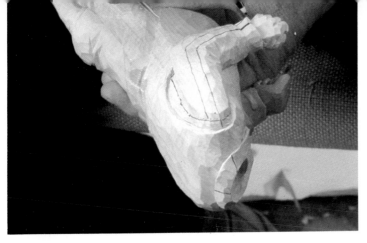

Keep adding stripes, moving from place to place. this way your stripe width is more likely to remain uniform. Set a good spacing between the strips, and keep that distance with the parallel lines.

The striped shirt.

As you think about colors you should consider the personality of the figure. Is he a sloppy dresser or a dandy? What would he wear? In this case I think our duffer would be neat and tend toward earthy colors.

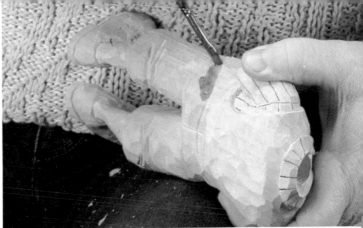

I'll start by painting the knickers with a burnt sienna wash. To mix my paints I use an empty juice jar. In the bottom I put about an inch of tube paint and fill the jar with turpentine. I can add more turpentine as needed. The paint settles so it needs to be shaken fairly regularly. This settling also lets us get more concentrated pigment when needed. Concentrated pigment also gathers on the lid for easy access. Begin by using a small brush to go around the top and bottom of the knickers where there is the most danger of the colors bleeding.

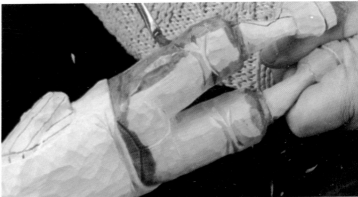

Switch to a bigger brush to finish the knickers.

Rub the knickers down to take off excess paint and even out the finish. If there is any heavily pigmented area that won't rub out, you can soak the cloth with a little turpentine.

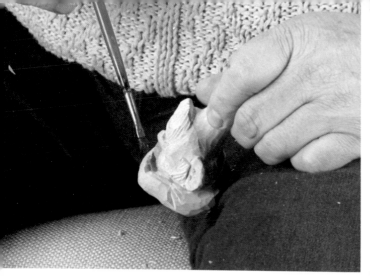

Next move to the cap which is also to be burnt sienna. Paint around the bottom where the cap meets the head.

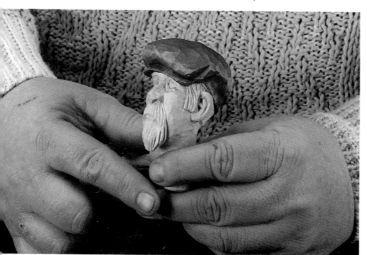

Finish the cap and wipe it off.

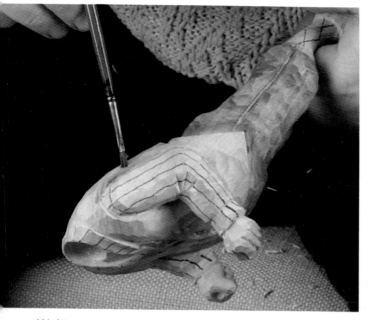

We'll use raw sienna for the sweater vest, again starting at the edges.

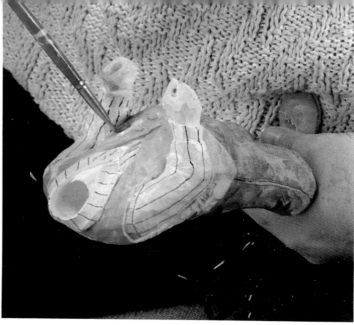

Fill in with the bigger brush.

Progress so far.

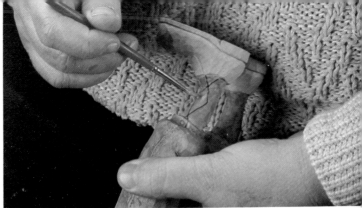

A bright blue seems appropriate for our friend. Use the same edging first method as before.

A gold color is added to the diamonds of the argyle socks, producing a greenish gold color. While adding colors over colors is a somewhat "iffy" way of doing patterns, it generally produces better results than trying to do the patterns separately. That almost always produces an unattractive error.

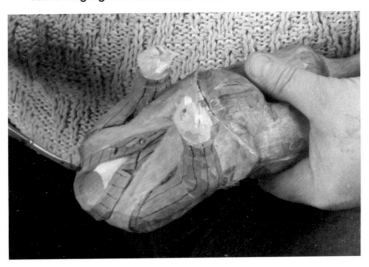

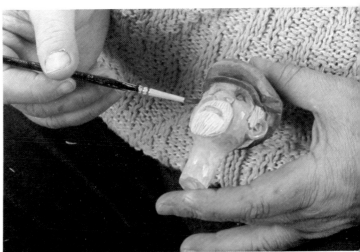

The shirt nears completion.

Next, paint the flesh area of the face. You don't need to worry about going over the eyes, since the white and iris color should cover nicely. The flesh tone I use is made by adding a little raw sienna to a commercial flesh tone. This takes away the pink color commercial flesh paints tend to be.

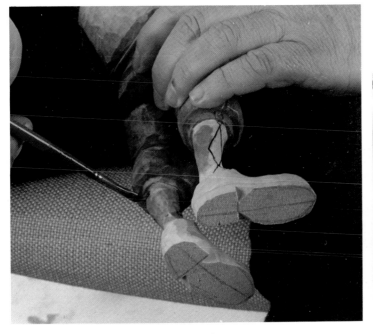

Use the same blue on the sock.

Use some red to add blush to the face. Put a little dots on the tip of the nose, the cheeks, ears, and lips.

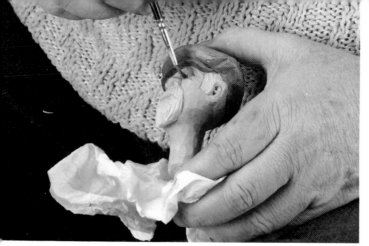

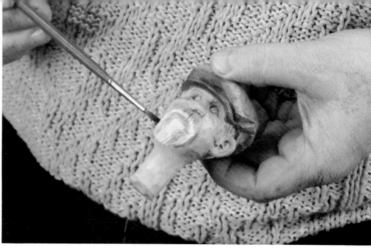

Wipe your brush off and dry brush the dots to blend the red color into the face.

We will paint a base coat of raw sienna on the hair and parts of the beard and then cover over it with white. This will give the impression of a man whose hair is gradually turning white.

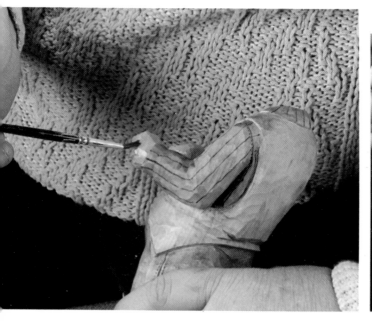

Paint the hands with the flesh tone.

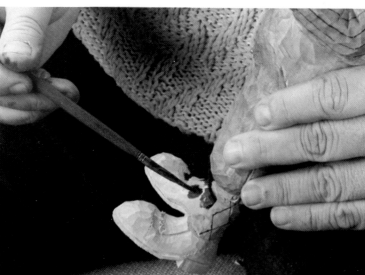

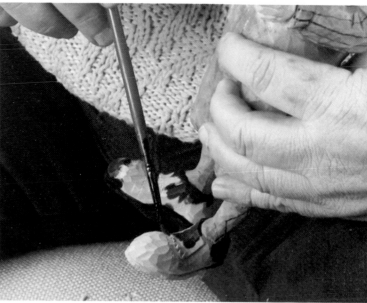

Add a little red to the back of the hands to give them more color.

The shoes are painted black. I don't often do a totally black shoe, usually preferring a two-toned shoe.

The painted shoes.

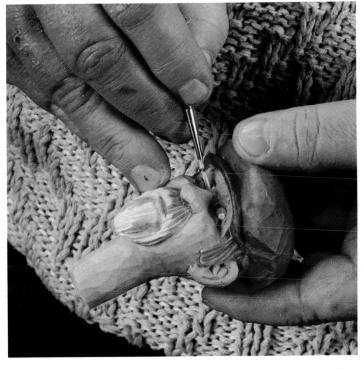

Apply white paint to the eyeballs using a fine brush. Be sure to get in the corners.

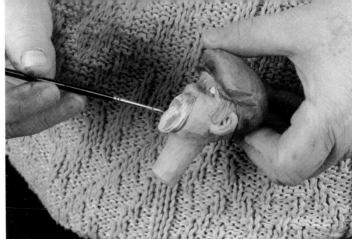

Apply white to the beard, allowing the sienna to show through...

giving this appearance after blending.

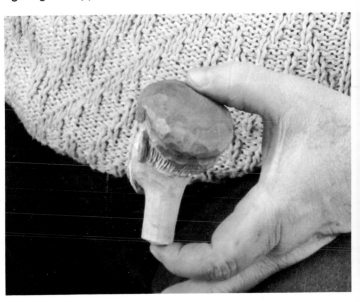

Continue applying white to the hair and sideburns.

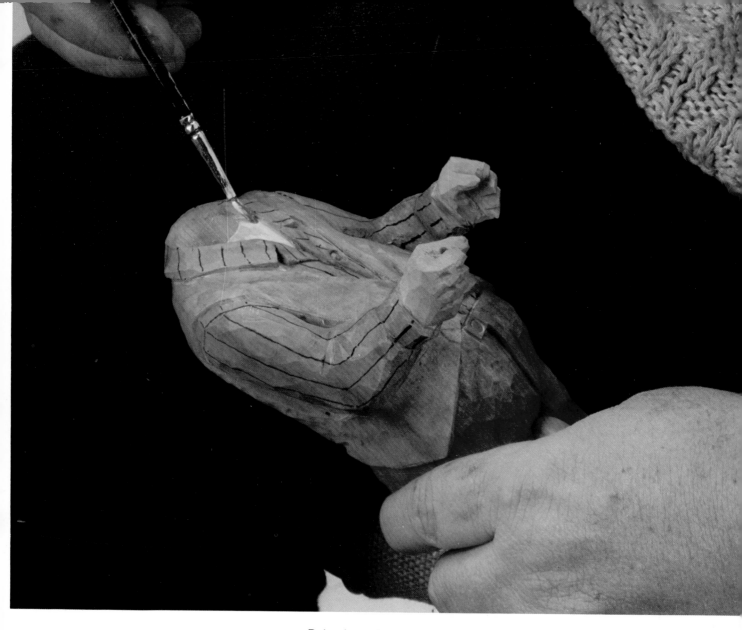

Paint the t-shirt white.

Redefine the irises of the eyes with the nailset. This will help in the painting.

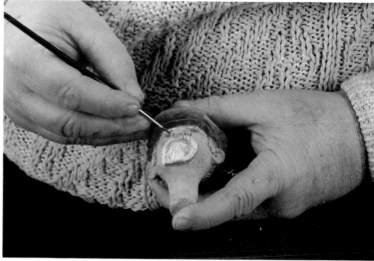

Use aquamarine blue to color the eyes, using a fine brush.

The eyes with the blue applied. Let this sit for awhile before applying the black to the pupils and a white glint.

Draw graph lines on the paper to simulate a scorecard.

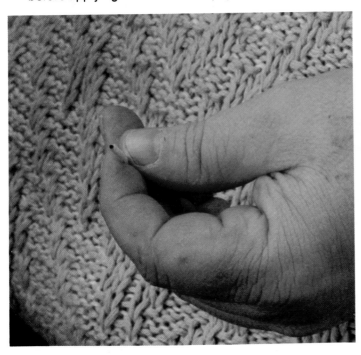

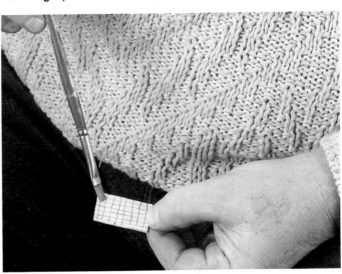

Paint the scorecard thin white wash.

Use a pen to color the lead of the pencil black.

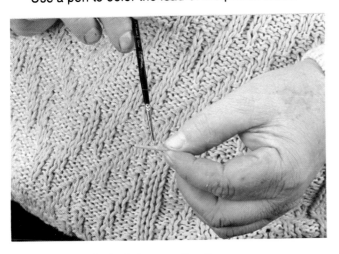

Paint the shaft of the pencil yellow.

Blot the excess paint with a towel.

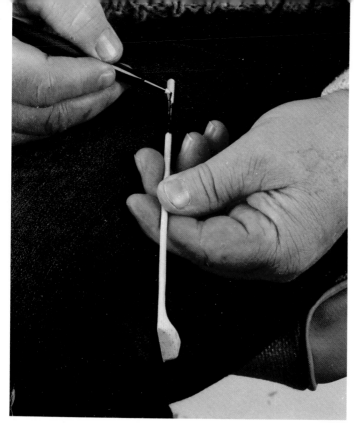

Put black on the golf club with the marking pen or with paint. Do the handle...

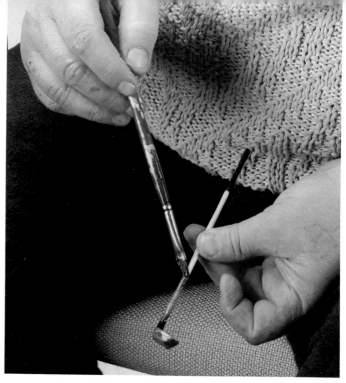

Paint the rest of the club with burnt sienna, wiping off the excess.

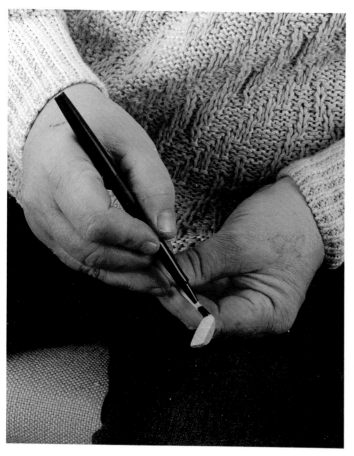

and the collar above the club head, which is usually done with string.

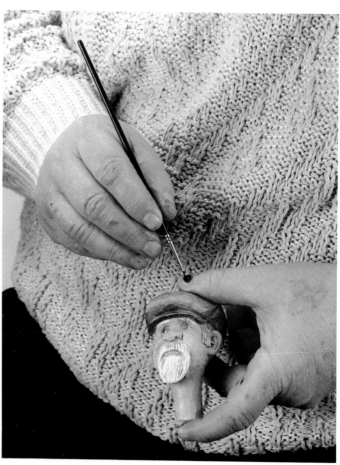

Now put a pupil in the eye using the finest tipped-brush you've got and concentrated pigment of black paint. For very fine work, I usually use the nail of my thumb as a little palette.

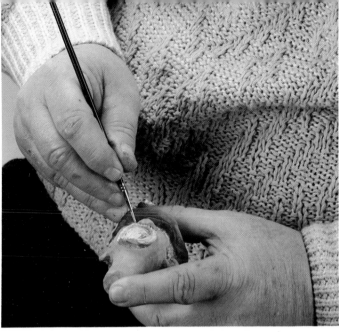

Apply the paint to the center of the eye.

A small glint of white in the eye brings it to life.

You can put it anywhere on the eyeball, but it has to be the same on both eyes.

The painted scorekeeper. The head is not yet glued and
by turning it the figure will take on a different character.

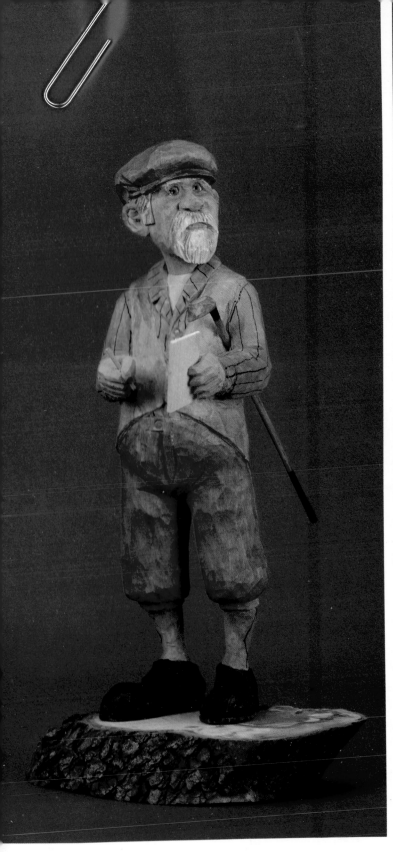

Formal shots of our golfer

Other members of the foursome.

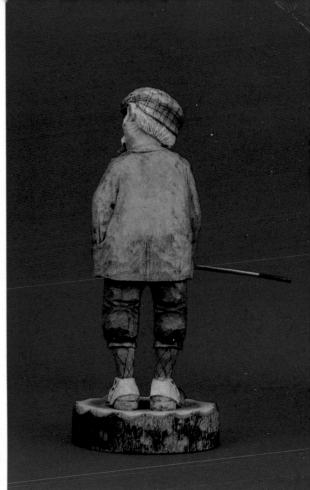

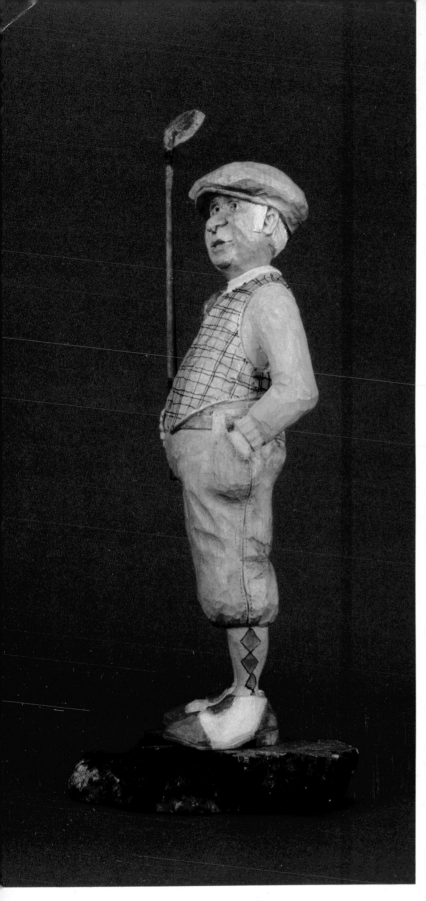

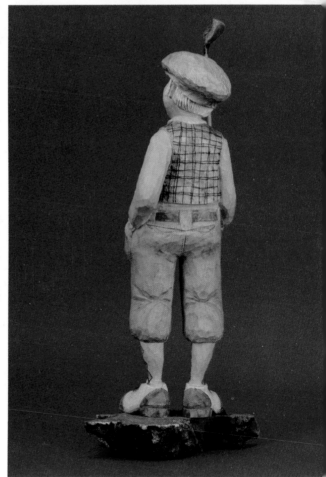

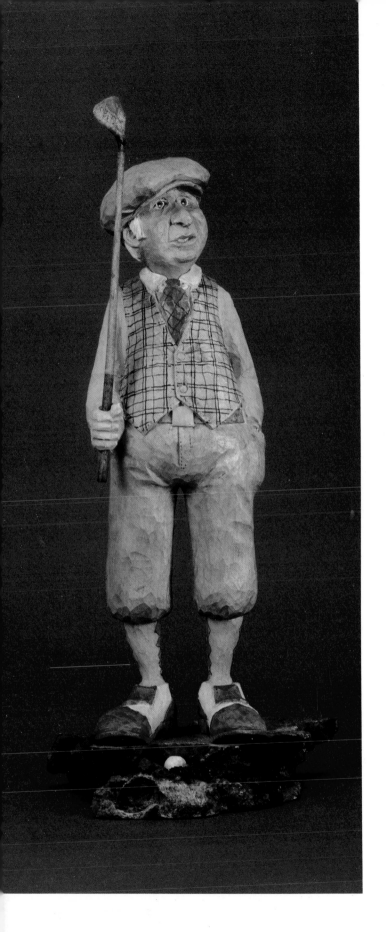

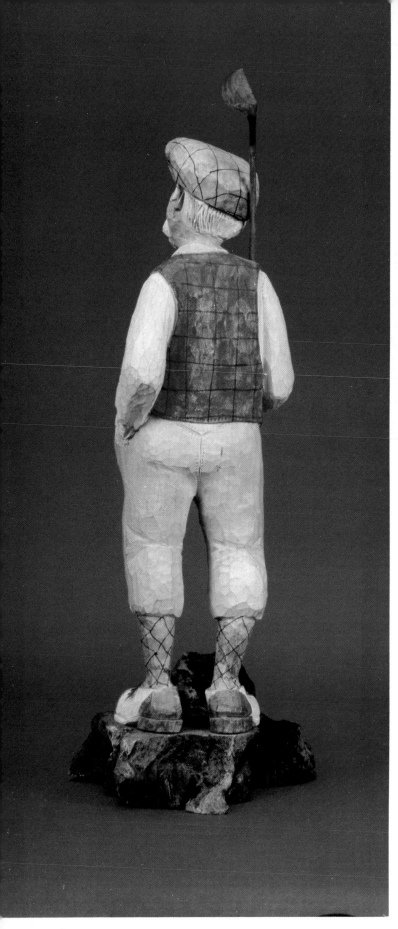

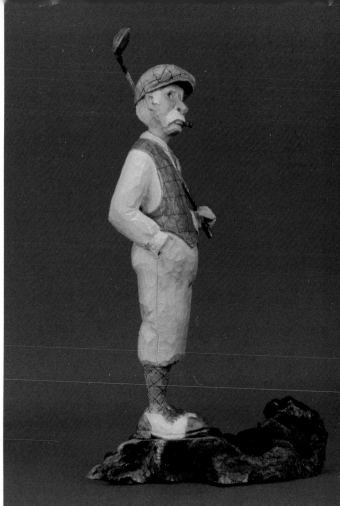

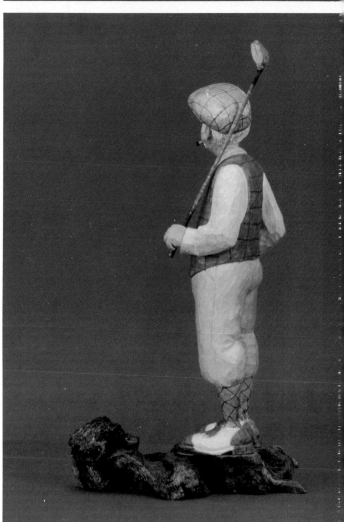